SKYSPLITTER FANFARE

BRIAN BALMAGES

INSTRUMENTATION

1	Conductor Score
8	Flute
2	Oboe
2	Bassoon
10	B♭ Clarinet
2	B♭ Bass Clarinet
4	E♭ Alto Saxophone
2	B♭ Tenor Saxophone
2	E♭ Baritone Saxophone
8	B♭ Trumpet
4	F Horn
4	Trombone

2	Euphonium
2	Baritone T.C.
4	Tuba
2	Timpani
2	Bells
2	Chimes (opt. Vibraphone)
2	Percussion 1 (Snare Drum, Bass Drum)
2	Percussion 2 (Crash Cymbals, Suspended Cymbal)
2	Percussion 3 (Low Tom, Floor Tom)

SUPPLEMENTAL and WORLD PARTS
Available for download from
www.alfred.com/supplemental

E♭ Alto Clarinet
E♭ Contra Alto Clarinet
B♭ Contra Bass Clarinet
E♭ Horn
Trombone in B♭ T.C.
Trombone in B♭ B.C.
Euphonium in B♭ B.C.
Tuba in B♭ T.C.
Tuba in B♭ B.C.
Tuba in E♭ T.C.
Tuba in E♭ B.C.
String Bass

Alfred

THE COMPOSER

Brian Balmages is known worldwide as a composer and conductor who equally spans the worlds of orchestral, band, and chamber music. His music has been performed by groups ranging from professional symphony orchestras to elementary schools in venues such as Carnegie Hall, the Kennedy Center, Sydney Opera House, Toronto Centre for the Arts, and many more. He is a recipient of the A. Austin Harding Award from the American School Band Directors Association, won the 2020 NBA William D. Revelli Composition Contest with his work *Love and Light*, and is an elected member of the prestigious American Bandmasters Association. Balmages was awarded the inaugural James Madison University Distinguished Alumni Award from the School of Visual and Performing Arts. In the same year, he was commissioned by his other alma mater, the University of Miami, to compose music for the inauguration of the institution's 6th president, Dr. Julio Frenk. His music was also performed as part of the 2013 Presidential Inaugural Prayer Service, which was attended by both President Obama and Vice President Biden.

As a conductor, Mr. Balmages enjoys regular engagements with all-state and regional ensembles as well as university and professional groups throughout the world. Notable guest conducting appearances have included the Midwest Clinic, Western International Band Clinic, Maryborough Music Conference (Australia), College Band Directors Conference, American School Band Directors Association National Conference, numerous state ASTA conferences, Teatro dell'Aquila (Italy), and others. Currently, he is Director of MakeMusic Publications and Digital Education for Alfred Music and MakeMusic.

ABOUT THE MUSIC

Back in 2009, I wrote a piece called *Starsplitter Fanfare* for band director Susan Nystoriak and the Beekmantown Elementary School Band in West Chazy, New York. It has since become an extremely popular work for bands all over the world, yet I can still remember the energy radiating from the kids as we performed the world premiere to a room full of excited families and friends.

Fast forward 13 years later, and I received a note from Susan:

"I hope you are well. I was wondering if you might be interested in doing another commissioned work for my students… A fanfare-like piece, similar to *Starsplitter Fanfare*, for a young band."

And thus, *Skysplitter Fanfare* was born. The piece is quite powerful and utilizes a big percussion section. (See options below if you have a smaller section. The piece still works quite well!) The driving rhythms in the percussion provide the momentum of the piece, which, despite being at a quicker tempo for beginners, is quite achievable as the winds do not have any eighth notes. I view this piece as a gateway for young musicians. A bridge from the method book to the performance music they will see later in their musical journeys. As I was writing the piece, I wanted this experience to be huge for them. I was hoping to give them a taste of what band can be like if they keep playing. I explore various textures and harmonies, and even some basic independent part writing (between sections) to get them motivated and fully engaged. The result was more than I could have hoped for, and I hope you enjoy the piece as much as I did while writing it!

PERCUSSION CONSIDERATIONS

For groups with large percussion sections, this piece can easily use 9 players without any doubling. Directors with even more students can double the Chimes part on Vibraphone, double Bells on other mallet instruments, and easily double Percussion 3 on other drums without snare (as long as they do not overpower the winds).

For smaller sections, the piece will work with just Percussion 1 (Snare Drum/Bass Drum) and Percussion 2 (Crash Cymbals/Suspended Cymbal)—and even less if need be. The Timpani part is completely optional, but certainly adds a lot if you have a player. Chimes and Percussion 3 are also completely optional. Regarding mallets, I prefer the Bells over Chimes if a decision needs to be made, primarily because of their importance in the section beginning at measure 21.

—Brian Balmages

DURATION: 1:30

commissioned by the Beekmantown Middle School Band
West Chazy, New York; Susan Nystoriak, Director

SKYSPLITTER FANFARE

BRIAN BALMAGES
(ASCAP)

Scan to
interact

37
Fl.
Ob.
Cl.
B. Cl.
div.
A. Sax.
T. Sax.
B. Sax.
37
Tpt.
Hn.
Bsn. / Tbn. / Euph.
Tuba
Timp.
Bls.
Ch.
Perc. 1
Perc. 2
Perc. 3
37
38
39
40
41